Limericks:
Too Gross

By Isaac Asimov and John Ciardi

A Grossery of Limericks

Limericks: Too Gross

Limericks: Too Gross

*   *   *

Isaac Asimov
and
John Ciardi

W·W·Norton & Company · New York London

Copyright © 1978 by W. W. Norton & Company, Inc.
Published simultaneously in Canada by Penguin Books Canada Ltd,
2801 John Street, Markham, Ontario L3R 1B4.
Printed in the United States of America.

First published as a Norton paperback 1985

Library of Congress Cataloging in Publication Data
Asimov, Isaac, 1920–
    Limericks, too gross.
    1. Limericks.   I. Ciardi, John, 1916–
joint author.   II. Title.
PN6231.L5A85   811'.5'4   78-13279

ISBN 0-393-04530-7 PBK.

W. W., Norton & Company, Inc.,
500 Fifth Avenue, New York, N.Y. 10110
W. W. Norton & Company Ltd.,
37 Great Russell Street, London WC1B 3NU

      6   7   8   9   0

To John
  I hope I didn't make you look too bad

—ISAAC

To Isaac
  Eat your heart out

—JOHN

Contents

Foreword I
by John Ciardi

* * *

Isaac Asimov and the Art of the Limerick

There is some bond between limerick and the English language that seems as natural as the bond between a clam and a sandy sea bottom, as if one had been specifically fitted to the other by the long tunings of evolution. Yet the limerick is a relatively recent form, and probably not even native to English. The first known specimens date from the early eighteenth century, and they are in French.

The Irish Brigade served in France from 1691 to about

1780. Its officers may have imported the form to Limerick in Ireland, whence the name of the form. Alternatively, the name may derive from the carousers' refrain "Will you come up to Limerick?" This refrain was once sung in chorus by the assembled drunkards after one among them had sung a solo verse. The solo need not have been a limerick as we know it. Perhaps it was sung to a roughly similar form. Perhaps it was even common at one time to sing limericks. Or perhaps not. Everything about the origin of the limerick—like Isaac Asimov's metric—is just a touch uncertain.

Yet one thing is sure. The form has survived many curious impositions in its brief history, and it will survive Isaac's. I have appended my own gross of limericks to this collection primarily to show that the form is not dead, though any reader who starts at the beginning of this book will find cause enough to fear for the limerick's life.

Like most growing things, the limerick had to suffer an age of innocence. It was Edward Lear (1812–1888) who tuned it to sweet nonsense, though usually with a hobbled last line in the manner of:

> There was a young man of Quebec
> Who stood in snow up to his neck.
>> When asked, "Ain't you friz?"
>> He replied, "Yes, I is.
> But we don't call this cold in Quebec."

Neither do we call it a limerick today. The true form absolutely demands that third rhyme, and (as I have tried to explain to a high-speed typist named Isaac who plays incessant literary chopsticks on three IBM Selectrics at once) what it demands is that the rhyme be both deft and outrageous. This typist has never found it hard to be outrageous. Unfortunately, he learned his deftness by rule of thumbs— ten of them.

It is for that reason that I have just sent him to the blackboard to copy out the following classic limerick fifty times, wiping the slate clean between each careful copy. As an exception to his fixed rule, I have insisted that he take time to think about what he is writing. No one who writes as he does can take time to think, and I am afraid my insistence may slow him down, but he will learn that I mean only to improve his writing habits. Here is the limerick:

> There was a young lady from Chichester
> Whose beauty made saints in their niches stir.
>> One morning at matins
>> Her breast in rose satins
> Made the bishop of Chichester's britches stir.

Alternatively, he may write the last rhyme as *brichester*.

. . . *Go ahead, Isaac. I will be speaking to these nice people while you keep usefully busy.* . . .

Something in the tutelary spirit of the limerick soon took it from Lear to leer. It can still romp among the innocent, but it is naturally drawn to rolling about with the satyrs, or among the satyric fantasies of the drunken.

So it was that Victorian and post-Victorian Britains of donnish tastes, suffering from the great gray queen's plague of inhibitions, seized upon the limerick as a more or less sanctioned way of venting all the four-letter words they had stored up as schoolboys. I suspect, though I cannot prove, that limericks of this sort tend to be British. The following specimen is certainly British:

> On the bank sat the bishop of Buckingham.
> He was cooling his balls—he was ducking 'em.
>   While observing the stunts
>   Of the cunts in the punts
> And the tricks of the pricks as was fucking 'em.

And certainly this one:

> Said the dowager duchess at tea,
> "Young man, do you fart when you pee?"
>   I replied, "Not a bit.
>   Do you belch when you shit?"
> —Which I'd say left the honours with me.

The following limerick, on the other hand—with "cold comfort" as one of the choicest locutions in the whole range of English poetry—cannot fail to be American:

> Said a widow whose singular vice
> Was to keep her dead husband on ice,
>   "It's been hard since I lost him.
>   I'll never defrost him.
> Cold comfort, but cheap at the price."

Let me say within hearing of that person at the blackboard, gentle readers, that I have no thought of taking all Americans to be subtle wits, nor of taking all Britains to be four-letter scalawags. I have known several Britains who were as approximately witty as science-fiction writers. Nor can one afford to be randomly snobbish, especially one who collaborates as indiscriminately as I do.

Whether or not the distinction is national, there is the limerick (and it can be very good) that serves mostly as an outlet for all the no-no words, and there is, on the other hand, the limerick honed to the subtleties of "single entendre."

One or the other, or both at once, the limerick naturally turns into a *roman à cleft*, and in the twentieth century its most natural habitat in America has been the Saturday night faculty swozzle led by the sots of the English Department.

The limerick has become a passion of academic drunkards to such an extent that even a fat ex-biochemist retooled as a universal genius has dared offer himself as a limericker— and without even the excuse of being an alcoholic. He is in fact a teetotaler.

Somewhere beyond the last space warp, where the ultimate parsec starts to curve back from beyond time, I shall have to stand before my tribal gods and explain to them how I came to associate with a teetotaler. I may then argue that the fellow's behavior is so naturally besotted that one tends to think of him as a drunkard, though the spirit is not in him. In better conscience, I could certainly argue that I have drunk enough for any two and that I have sought to assign my excess of merit to him, for it is only natural that such hack writers seek increase in association with the more spiritedly literate. And I shall infallibly point out as his saving graces, first, that he is a dirty old man, and second, that he has renounced academe. For reasons known only to his own hard-clutched psyche, he has insisted on retaining the title of his tenure, and is still an in-name-only Associate Professor of Biochemistry at Boston University, which can no longer bid for his services against the rates now available to selected speed-typists who manage to persuade editors that such typing is an act of genius.

I shall, finally, plead long friendship. We are both native Bostonians. I knew him when even he wasn't entirely sure he was a genius. I have grown to depend upon him as the penitential soul depends upon its hair shirt. Any one hour in the wind tunnel of this man's wit, I am persuaded, will release me from a century of future purgatorial pain—if I am not dragged beyond salvation by ill-chosen companions.

As a test of my piety and forebearance, I have even forced myself to endure his pretensions to the ministry of the True Limerick. I will not go so far as to say he has profaned it. It would be more accurate to say he has propaned it. Or dieseled it. Hell, I think, will turn out to be diesel-powered. Isaac has obviously been having a hell of a time with the limerick, for once he is through grinding its gears, it never fails to give off the attar of a New York City bus on a muggy day.

The limerick—as I hope he may yet learn by consulting the truly written second half of this book—is a subtler and less noisy thing. I am not entirely convinced the art of it is entirely beyond him. Given such example, I don't see why even he could not learn. For he is conscientious. His work at the blackboard, for instance, has been. . . .

But why is he adding all those footnotes? Just look at what he has done:

Chichester. Earlier *Cisseceaster.* The second element, *chester*, derives from Latin *castra*, fortified place. The first element is probably from *Cissa,* also known as *Cissi,* son of Aelli (whoever he was). Note that with Old English "c" sounded as a kappa, the original name was pronounced approximately "kissy keester"— a delicious subtlety, for though only the young lady's breasts are overtly stated to have enflamed His Worship, the very place name, with all the delicacy and force of a subliminal suggestion, introduces her *kissy keester* as a further source of the bishop's lay impulse.

What drivel! I can only suppose he has been reading some of those heavy-handed collections in which the limerick is reduced to little more than a vehicle for arch footnotes. Was it Norman Douglas ("South Wind" Douglas) who started this fashion? His early under-the-counter collection smothered the limerick in such stuff in much the way the local greasy spoon smothers liver with onions, to disguise a questionable taste. Or is it only that the limerick has been taken over by academics who have brought to it their habit of living as footnotes to their own psyches? It won't do. Excuse me. I must put an end to this once and . . .

—*No, Isaac. The first commandment is: Thou shalt not commit felonious footnotery. Come now, there is no need to sulk. Yes, alas, I love you. But is it love if everything must be explained in footnotes? Erase them, I say.*

—*There. See for yourself how nicely it does without such stuff.*

—*Of course, I have faith in you. Once you have learned to read, there is no end to what you might not overachieve. Yes, I know you have been so busy writing that you haven't had time to become literate. But just take things one at a time. And the first thing to learn about the limerick is that it must stand on its own or it just can't stand.*

Why don't you start by reading to me what you have written on the blackboard? —Sorry. I forgot you can't read. What? You'll write me a limerick instead? A whole gross of them? Oh, I see: you want me to turn the page and read what you have written so you can hear how it sounds. Suppose I skip to the back of the book and read some real limericks to you? You'd rather hear your own. Well, why not? I, too, was a professor once—a Full Professor, of course—and I always took pleasure in the challenge offered by what used to be called the "unusual" student.

You point to the words, and I will say them for you. But first, please excuse me, while I apologize to what readers you haven't frightened away. You turn the page and find the place. I'll be right with you.

. . . Sorry, dear reader. Please forgive the interruption. I shall be delighted to have you join our reading, if you care to stay. But let me beg you to understand about Isaac. He is a self-made man and a remarkable one. He has, in fact, some remark or other on every known subject, and on several unknown ones. But being self-made is a bit like turning out your own picture frames. They come out square enough, and they look fine from a distance, but once you come close enough to examine the miters, you understand how much difference a touch of professionalism could have made.

To change metaphors, since we are inviting you to some sort of feast, I am afraid the wine you will be starting with won't qualify as a true vintage. Yet it is a zesty little wine, ordinary but pert, and pleasantly brash in its own way. At least try it.

Once it is out of the way, I can promise you your choice of a dozen dozen from Bacchus's own cellar.

Chin-chin,

John Ciardi
Bill Nimmo's Bar
Metuchen, N.J.

Foreword II

by Isaac Asimov

＊　　　＊　　　＊

John Ciardi and the Art of the Foreword

There are those (John Ciardi among them) who say that John Ciardi has written children's poetry that can't be better; that he has done a translation of Dante that all but improves on the original; that he has a voice that can read even the telephone book and make it sound beautiful; but I—

I have always held John Ciardi to be the very model of behavior and the pink of deportment. All should behold the man and observe him narrowly, for whatever he does, why do the contrary and you will be *right*.

Some people fall short of perfection most of the time, but John Ciardi never does. Without fail, without exception, without swerving to either right or left a hair's-breadth, he invariably does the perfectly wrong thing.

With all that in mind, I read his Foreword, the same one you have just skipped. Since he was long, verbose, and muddy, I shall be brief, terse, and luminously clear. Since he was heavy-handed and quoted filthy limericks he did not write, I will be deft and quote clean limericks that I did write. I shall quote three of them, in fact, and all about John Ciardi:

1. To make friends with the lumpish John Ciardi
   Needs a spirit uncouth, rough, and hardy.
       When in line for a bit
       Of amusement and wit—
   Did he get it? Why, no, he was tardy.

2. To a dinner arrived fat John Ciardi
   With only his appetite hearty.
       Conversational ploys?
       He had nothing but noise,
   And he spoiled every bit of the party.

3. What more shall I say of John Ciardi?
   His humor is junk, his wit shoddy.
       To speak of his mind
       Would be most unkind
   And, God, would you look at that body.

There you are, John. It took you many pages to decide you had finally managed to deflate me. The job of deflating you is far easier.

                                                    Isaac Asimov

Limericks:
A Gross

by Isaac Asimov

*   *   *

1. POLITENESS

Breathed a tender young man from Australia,
"My darling, please let me unveilia,
    And then, oh, my own,
    If you'll kindly lie prone,
I'll endeavor, my sweet, to impalia.

2. DUCKBILL PLATYPUS

"We refuse," said two men from Australia,
"Bestiality this saturnalia.
    For now, we bethink us,
    The ornithorhynchus
Is our down-under type of Mammalia."

3. EDWARDIAN

Lady Gwendolyn, skirts all a-rustle,
Resisted and put up a tussle,
    But the wicked old earl
    With his fingers a-curl
At last managed a pinch on the bustle.

4.   A MERE TRIFLE

Said a certain young man with a grin,
"I think it is time to begin."
    Said the girl with a sneer,
    "With what? Why, your pee-er
Is scarcely as big as a pin."

5.   WITH MEAT SAUCE

There was a young woman named Betty
Who thought waterbeds rather petty.
    The results were less hasty,
    She thought, and more tasty,
If one screwed on a bed of spaghetti.

6.   APOSTATE

There once was a daring young Jew
Who said to his rabbi, "Screw you,
    I eat meat on Yom Kippur
    Mixed with milk by the dipper,
And as for the shiksehs—woo, woo!"

7.   SHE KNOWS WHAT SHE WANTS

There was a young woman of Essex
Who had many occasions to bless sex
    And would banish from sight
    Any moron who might
Suggest it was time she had less sex.

8.   ONLY NATURAL

A young nun from Long Beach, California,
Said, "I think it's important to warnia
    That though seeming a saint
    I've an awful complaint,
I am just getting steadily hornia."

9.   BIG MOUTH

Said young Joseph to beautiful Nadya,
"It's many long years since I hadya."
    Said she, "You're a rat
    To talk about that.
Why can't you keep secrets, you cadya?"

10. BIOLOGY

Said an ovum one night to a sperm,
"You're a very attractive young germ.
    Come join me, my sweet,
    Let our nuclei meet
And in nine months we'll both come to term."

11. THE HORRORS OF DRINK

When a certain young woman named Terry
Got drunk on a small sip of sherry
    She'd insist upon games
    With embarrassing names
Not in any refined dictionary.

12. THERE SHE GOES

There is a young lass of Valencia
For whom sex is a form of dementia.
    For the first hour she's quiet
    Then she builds to a riot
With a noise that grows quickly intensia.

13. SEEK AND YE SHALL FIND

Said a certain young girl of Madrid
Who kept her vagina well hid,
    "For a lousy peseta,
    I am no fornicata,
But I'll spread for an adequate bid."

14. TIME INDEED

"It is time," said a woman from Devon,
"To exchange maiden bliss for sex heaven.
    There is music, it's spring,
    Flowers bloom, birdies sing;
And besides I've just turned thirty-seven."

15. FRIGID

There's a beautiful woman named Pam
Whose sexy appearance is sham
    When a man wants a lay
    She yawns and says, "Nay!"
And he stands there frustrated. God damn!

16. IT'S TRUE

There's a certain young woman named Janet
Who's the sexiest dish on the planet.
　　From her toe to her palm
　　She's a nuclear bomb
And no one, thank God, wants to ban it.

17. MUSICAL CHAIRS

There was a young fellow named Hal
Whose wife ran away with his pal.
　　He abhorred deprivation
　　So he found consolation
In the arms of another friend's gal.

18. PRIDE

At a nudist camp, sweet little Lillian
Was slated to lead the cotillion.
　　This made her so proud
　　That to shine in the crowd
She painted her nipples vermilion.

19. GRAMMAR

"Adultery," said Joseph, "is nice.
If once is all right, better twice.
    This doubling of rations
    Improves my sensations
For the plural of spouse, friend, is spice."

20. TOO FAT

Said a woman from Richmond, Virginia,
"I'd be rich if I only were skinnia.
    If I lost thirty pounds
    The boys would have grounds
To say, 'How I'd pay to be inia.' "

21. OH, YEAH?

A prim Texan, when caught in sin's vortex,
Would mutter, "Let go of that whore, Tex.
    You must never employ her
    You don't really enjoy her
All that pleasure is just in your cortex."

22. NOTHING TO IT

A young woman, polite and demure,
Would reform the depraved and impure.
    She found it a breeze
    And did it with ease
For her work was a mere sinecure.

23. FRUSTRATION

There was an old fellow from Anchorage
Who was riddled with fury and rancorage.
    When he offered abusement
    The girls gave refusement
And all he was left with was hankerage.

24. SEA DOG

A captain, exposed to alarms
And much given to shivers and qualms,
    Just couldn't keep warm
    On a boat in a storm
Without the first mate in his arms.

25. REALISM

There was a young fellow named Clark
Who decided that sex was a lark.
    Since he couldn't endure
    The sight of a whore
He would always make love in the dark.

26. HOW NICE

Said a guy to his gal, quite ambitiously,
"I will screw you, my dear, expeditiously."
    The lass simply smiled,
    Said, "Delightful! Just wild!"
And it all ended simply deliciously.

27. RIGHT, LEFT, RIGHT, LEFT

There was a young woman from Venice
Who's a regular sexual menace.
    She would hop from one boy
    To another, with joy,
Like a ball in a fast game of tennis.

28. ECONOMY

There's a man who is named Isidore
Who has never made love to a whore.
    It is not that he frowns
    At the ups and the downs;
He just thinks paying cash is a bore.

29. WHAT'S YOUR HURRY?

A certain young man was so deft
That he left his poor girl quite bereft.
    He'd put it in slickly
    Then pull it out quickly
And before she had felt it, he'd left.

30. MAY I HAVE THE HONOR?

There was a young woman named Suzie
Who was not much inclined to be choosy
    So that after a day
    Of intensive sex play
She was apt to remark, "Say, just who's he?"

31. IF

My boy, if you like to have fun,
If you take all the girls one by one,
    And when reaching four score
    Still don't find it a bore,
Why, then, you're a hero, my son.

32. MODERATION

There was an old fellow named Reese
Who longed to make love to his niece.
    Don't accuse him of gall,
    He did not expect all,
But just an occasional piece.

33. JUST POSSIBLY

Said a very attractive young Haitian,
"Please begin with a gentle palpation.
    If you do as I say
    In the way of sex play
Why, who knows, there may be fornication."

34. AIM LOW

A young fellow, with rueful veracity,
Said he hadn't much phallic capacity;
     So he tried no one new
     Stayed with girls he could screw,
And that's what I call perspicacity.

35. WRONG PLACE, WRONG TIME

There was a young fellow named Ned
Who'd invent comic verses in bed.
     In the end the poor simp
     Let his penis grow limp
And the woman beneath bashed his head.

36. ACCIDENT

I got into bed with Dolores
And her diaphragm proved to be porous.
     The result of our sins
     Was a fine pair of twins;
Now the birth control people abhor us.

37. DISAPPOINTMENT

A certain young fellow named Scott
Once jumped his young bride on their cot.
    He intended no shirking
    But from sheer overworking
A dry run is all that she got.

38. WHY, SISTER!

A young nun who made notes in her diary
That were terribly torrid and fiery
    Once left it behind
    For her abbess to find.
Now she isn't allowed in the priory.

39. FIT FOR A MARATHON

To the ancient Greek writer, Herodotus,
Said a pretty young thing, "My, how hard it is."
    Said he, "Do you fear
    I will hurt you, my dear?"
And she said, "Are you crazy? Thank God it is."

40. HOW CUTE!

Said Jane, "I just love to exhibit,
A delight I let nothing inhibit.
    I think it's a ball
    To undress and bare all.
Oh, I'm such a young flibbertigibbet."

41. GELATINOUS

There wasn't a soul with a fatter ass
Than a maiden who lived at Cape Hatteras.
    When stroked it would wiggle
    And shiver and jiggle.
Men lined up, by the score, just to pat 'er ass.

42. MUTTER, MUTTER

There was a young woman named Shirley
With eyes blue and cheeks pink and teeth pearly.
    Her figure curved nicely
    Where it ought to precisely,
And when she said, "No," men grew surly.

43.   TEMPORARY

There was a young lass named Theresa
Whom the fellows all longed for a piece o';
    But she isn't for sale
    To some lustful old male.
You can't buy 'er—but money will lease 'er.

44.   UNFAIR COMPETITION

There was a young fellow named Sturgis
Who needed a lass for his urges,
    But how could he buy
    With the price bid sky-high
By the men of the various clergies?

45.   DESPERATE

There's a certain young woman named Fran
Who has it whenever she can.
    But that's not really much
    So she's ripe for the touch
Of just any old warm-blooded man.

46. OH, DON'T TELL ME

A devout Jewish maiden named Donna
Is extremely afraid she's a goner.
    She was screwing one day
    In each possible way
Quite forgetting it was Rosh Hashana.

47. PRINCIPLES

There was once a remarkable stripper
Who'd undress to the very last zipper
    Before one—before all—
    But one day in the fall
She refused and said, "Not on Yom Kippur."

48. MIGHTY

There was a young fellow from Dallas
Who was rugged, enormous, and callous.
    He would shatter chrome steel
    With one blow of his heel
Then powder the bits with his phallus.

49. HOW GODLIKE

A man with a prick of obsidian,
Of a length that was truly ophidian,
    Was sufficiently gallant
    To please girls with his talent
Each day in the midpostmeridian.

50. IN ALPHABETICAL ORDER?

There was a young lover named Marius
Whose approaches to sex were quite various.
    He kept in his files
    All possible styles
That came under the head of nefarious.

51. HURRY!

At his wedding, a bridegroom named Crusoe
Was embarrassed to find his prick grew so.
    His eager young bride
    Pulled him quickly astride
And was screwed while still wearing her trousseau.

52. SOFTER SIDE

The haughty philosopher, Plato,
Would unbend to a sweet young tomato.
    Though she might be naive
    Like you wouldn't believe
He would patiently show her the way to.

53. CAUGHT!

Poor old John doesn't really do much;
Here and there just a fugitive touch.
    But his wife happened by
    When his palm stroked a thigh
Now the fellow is really in dutch.

54. PEEK-A-BOO

The excitement produced by Miss Whipple
Was very much more than a ripple.
    She was covered with clothes
    From her head to her toes
Save for delicate holes at each nipple.

55. ZZZZ

I'm afraid one can hardly suppose
A presence as boring as Joe's.
    When he's finally led
    A girl into bed
She promptly falls into a doze.

56. ANYTHING TO PLEASE

Bill maintains that he isn't inclined
To value a girl for her mind.
    But to help him get in
    He will do that and grin,
Though he'd rather admire her behind.

57. DISAPPOINTMENT

Said an angry young damsel, "What meanness!
First a fellow will brag of his penis,
    Then you say, 'Come on, lover,
    Why don't you uncover?'
And he does—and you're shocked at the wee-ness."

58.   EITHER WAY

Said a certain young fellow from Texas,
"You can't dream how extremely it vexes
    My mother that I,
    However I try,
Stay attracted to both of the sexes."

59.   THAT INDEFINABLE
      SOMETHING

"I'm falling in love with young Liz, ma!"
Said Johnny one morning to his ma.
    "Her breast size, you see
    Is 42-G
And that gives a woman charisma."

60.   CHÀCUN A SON GOUT

Said a certain young maid of Tortuga,
"How I wish I could mate with a cougar.
    The sheer joy of the matching
    Would be worth all the scratching."
But her friends think she's clearly meshuggah.

61. ALWAYS THE WAY

There once was a handsome young sheik
With a marvelous penile physique.
    Its length and its weight
    Made it seem really great
But he fell very short on technique.

62. IDENTIFICATION

Last night, a blind date phoned Amelia
And said, "I will wear a camellia.
    If you need something more
    You'll be satisfied for
I'm the one who'll at once get familiar."

63. OUCH!

There was once a young fellow named Nick,
Who was terribly proud of his prick.
    Without fear it would bend
    He would bounce on its end.
As he said, "It's my own pogostick."

64.   THE AYES HAVE IT

There was a fair woman named Kate
Who would prove such an excellent date
      That each fellow would note
      (A unanimous vote)
That she wasn't just fair—she was great!

65.   SLAVE OF DUTY

There once was a lazy young clerk
Who thought sex a great deal of work.
      But he said, "When I shove
      It's a labor of love,
And that sort of thing I can't shirk."

66.   FIRST THINGS FIRST

There's a certain young woman named Sharon
Who's decided to marry a baron.
      At age eighty-four
      He can do it no more.
But he's rich—so she isn't despairin'.

67. NO LUCK

To her mother said sorrowful Dagmar,
"My social life's simply a drag, ma.
　　Of my men, there are two
　　Who don't know how to screw
And the third is just simply a fag, ma."

68. VILLAGE IDIOT

There was a young fellow named Wayne
Who's too dumb to come out of the rain.
　　He has learned, more or less,
　　How to lift a girl's dress
More than that is too much for his brain.

69. SHIFTING GEARS

There's a certain erotic old bum
Whom no one can think of as dumb.
　　At the end of a bout
　　When his prick is worn out
He shifts to the use of his thumb.

70. SECRETIVE

A certain young girl of Bel Air
Once carefully braided the hair
    All over her crotch
    Letting nobody watch,
And the fellows all thought it unfair.

71. WHAT A RELIEF!

Said Wilma, "Last week I believed
I had slipped and had somehow conceived.
    My prayers were a myriad,
    And I then got my period,
And now, for a while, I'm reprieved."

72. NOT HER FAULT

Have you heard the incredible news
About Linda, who's off on a cruise?
    She had sex on the coral
    In ways most immoral
But John puts the blame on the booze.

73. DON'T LOSE THAT VOICE

There's an outlaw out there by El Paso
Who once dodged the old sheriff's thrown lasso.
      It was aimed for his nuts
      So good luck to the klutz.
To this day he is still singing basso.

74. A BIG IMPROVEMENT

A girl who was from Brooklyn Heights
Looked quite mediocre in tights.
      There was much more approval
      When, upon their removal,
She revealed more spectacular sights.

75. YES, MOTHER

There was a young girl from Bordeaux
Whose mother said, "Always say no!"
      But the girl said "No," *after*
      The fun, when with laughter,
She'd screwed her good friend, Pierrot.

76. ADVANTAGE

There once was a young spaced-out drummer
Who, everyone said, was no bummer.
    He needs but one stick
    And that is his prick
And his pounding's what makes him a comer.

77. SO THEY GOT WET

There was a young woman named Ella
Who was caught in the rain with a fella,
    But were both so intent
    On complete ravishment
They forgot to put up an umbrella.

78. FAILURE

A dignified fellow named Cliff
Got into a hell of a tiff
    With his eager young wife
    In their newlywed life
When only his manner proved stiff.

79.   HE'LL NEVER LEARN

There was an old fellow of Michigan
Who said, "Oh, I wish I were rich again,
      But each time I'm ahead
      I fall into the bed
Of that rotten old gold-digging bitch again."

80.   I WONDER WHY

Said a certain young fellow from Utah,
"I've a girl, but I don't seem to suitah.
      I am tall; I am wise;
      I've got lovely blue eyes;
And in matters of sex I am neutah."

81.   ENUNCIATION

An elderly sage of B'nai B'rith
Told his friend he was quite full of pith.
      This could mean "full of fact"
      And "with meaning compact,"
But not when you're lithping like thith.

82. TOO BAD

As a poet, a young man named Buck
Was utterly lacking in luck.
      He tried limericks (lecherous)
      But found rhyming quite treacherous
And to rhyme "Buck" and "luck" left him stuck.

83. GUESS WHAT!

To her lover said pretty young Julie,
"I don't want to alarm you unduly.
      I don't intend blame
      And yet, all the same,
You've produced a small pregnancy. —Truly!"

84. READY!

There was a young lady named Lynne
Who said, "I'm prepared to begin
      Any sort of activity
      That suits my proclivity
Provided it counts as a sin."

85. GET WITH IT!

Said a certain young woman named Amy,
"I am seeking a fellow to tame me
    And teach me the newer
    Mad routes to l'amour
For to stay virgin longer will shame me."

86. LET'S NOT WATCH

There is a young woman named Rose
Who has a fixation on toes.
    She thinks that love's remedies
    Start with pedal extremities,
And she then passes on to—God knows!

87. YUM, YUM!

A gourmet's delight is Priscilla
For her breath's a distinct sarsparilla.
    One breast tastes of thyme
    The other of lime
And her vaginal flavor's vanilla.

88. DON'T CROWD

There was a young woman from Paris
Whom nothing at all could embarrass,
    So when screwing at night
    She would turn on the light
For the audience out on the terrace.

89. FOR A CHANGE

There was a young woman named Joan
Who once had six men of her own.
    The first was for Mondays
    Then the rest—except Sundays
When she'd just masturbate all alone.

90. ONLY FAIR

There was a young Frenchman, Marceau,
Who said to his girlfriend, "Ah, no.
    I admit it is sweet,
    Ma très chère petite,
But it's your turn to move down below."

91. WAITING FOR LEFTY

A young man, quite well known to be deft,
Said, "My dear, do not feel so bereft.
    Though I've sprained my right hand
    I'm not really unmanned.
I can diddle quite well with my left."

92. AW, SHUCKS

A voluptuous girl named Elaine
Greeted all Joe's attempts with disdain.
    When he took her to dinner
    And tried to get in 'er,
Where he only got "in" was "in vain."

93. SO STOP ALREADY

There was a young girl named Priscilla
With whom sex proved completely a thrilla
    One just can't get enough
    Of that girl's kind of stuff
(Although the sixth time it's a killa).

94. MR. AMERICA

How they marvel at Joe's penal vigor,
At its size and magnificent rigor.
> When he was a lad
> 'Twas already not bad
And with age, it keeps on getting bigger.

95. SENSUAL PERCEPTION

There was a young man from Wilkes-Barre
Who, at following girls, was a star.
> His vision was poor,
> His hearing unsure,
But he sniffed pheromones from afar.

96. OH, APHRODITE

Said a chic and attractive young Greek,
"Would you like a quick peek that's unique?"
> "Why, yes," Joe confessed,
> So she quickly undressed
And showed him her sleek Greek physique.

97. WHY WASTE TIME?

Joe inspects girls with conscienceless suavity
In search of their luscious concavity,
    At which he will leap
    Like a wolf on a sheep
With utterly hardened depravity.

98. CAN'T TRUST THE BLOKE

While sleeping, a sailor from Twickenham
Was aware of a strange object stickenham.
    Before he could turn
    He'd occasion to learn
His shipmate was plunging his prickenham.

99. SAFETY FIRST

There once was a haughty old baronet
With a prick twice as long as a clarinet.
    If the thing ever dangled
    'Twould be stepped on and mangled,
So he kept it tucked inside a hair-i-net.

100. MODESTY

There was once an athletic young jock
Who could shatter large rocks with his cock,
    But a coed said, "Dear,
    Please insert the thing here."
And he fainted away with the shock.

101. CHOICE

Said Joe of a woman named Alison
"That's a lady with whom I would dally, son.
    For her body, you see,
    Is indubitably,
Where I'd like to deposit my phallus on."

102. ON TARGET

There was a young woman named Sally
Who loved an occasional dally.
    She sat on the lap
    Of a well-endowed chap
And said, "Ooo, you're right up my alley."

103. PRACTICAL

There was a young fellow named Si
Whose motto was "Never say die."
    Too plain to attract,
    He never attacked.
If he couldn't persuade, he would buy.

104. PLUG

A new volume of verse Asimovian
That's replete with a humor that Jovian
    Represents stimulation
    That will prove the occasion
For a laughing response quite Pavlovian.

105. DISAPPOINTMENT

There was a young woman name Jeannie
Who sobbed to her date, "You're a meanie.
    You claim you're a stud,
    But, oh, what a dud!
Your prick is a real teeny-weeny."

106. LUXURIANT

The dark pubic hair of young Sadie
Is the longest you'll find on a lady.
    You must guess at the angle
    When you push through that tangle,
But once there, the surroundings are shady.

107. MALFRAGRANCE

There was an old fellow named Eric
Whose breath made those near him choleric.
    He produced a hiatus,
    In crowds, with his flatus.
He's a one-man disease, atmospheric.

108. SKIN-DEEP

There's a woman whose name is Lucille
Who, whenever she chooses to peel,
    Discloses a skin
    One would love to get in
For the sake of its wonderful feel.

109. SECOND BEST, I'M AFRAID

Said Joe, "When I leave my young Stephanie
Her cries of unhappiness deafen me,
But I make no apology,
I rely on technology,
And screw her by wireless telephony."

110. SO DID BORIS GODUNOV

The eminent basso, Chaliapin,
Loved the sound of an audience clappin'.
But that tuneful go-getter
Loved one thing even better:
Spending few hours in bed simply nappin'.

111. NOT EASY

There was a young fellow named Paul
Whose prick was exceedingly small.
When in bed with a lay
He could screw her all day
Without touching the vaginal wall.

112. BITER BIT

Joe invited his girl to dutch treat,
Which sweetened the old balance sheet.
    Though he saved lots of dough,
    The next night proved a blow
When he could not arouse her to heat.

113. EASY GOING

A woman there was named Pauline
Who's always been terribly keen
    On kissing and wooing—
    Indiscriminate screwing—
And anything else that's obscene.

114. FALSE ADVERTISING

There was a young fellow named Barney
Who wanted to visit Killarney.
    He was told the colleens there
    Were screwing machines there
But found that was Irishmen's blarney.

115. GOOD FIT

"Near my girl," said a lecher named Cecil,
"Is the place where I usually nestle.
    Nothing else is a patch
    On the way that we match.
She's the mortar and I am the pestle."

116. WHAT A WASTE

There once was a woman named Baker,
A thoughtful and pious young Quaker.
    She's terrifically stacked
    But the tragical fact
Is that none of the fellows can make 'er.

117. DAYDREAM

Said a certain old lecher named Day,
"If my good wife would but go away,
    I'd locate a young lass
    And then let the world pass
And I'd do what comes natural and play."

1 1 8. GOOD THINKING

There was a fan-dancer of Cannes
Who developed an excellent plannes
    For a lecherous dance
    Without any pants
And some very big holes in the fannes.

1 1 9. YOU CAN'T HAVE EVERYTHING

Daphne's looks are completely imperial
And her style of lovemaking's ethereal.
    She's erotically active
    And intensely attractive.
What a shame her disease is venereal!

1 2 0. SHOCKING

Comic verse of the type that's limerical
Prove to be, often times, anticlerical.
    A saintly old minister
    Is depicted as sinister
And as filled with a lust quite hysterical.

121. WATCH IT

There was an old fellow of Tripoli
Who used to make love rather nippily.
    Said his angry young lass
    While rubbing her ass,
"Less teethily, please, and more lippily."

122. VERSATILE

Shyly said a young woman named Mabel,
"How delighted I am that I'm able
    To screw on a bed
    —Or a sofa instead
—Or the grass—or the floor—or the table."

123. ELIZABETHAN

That old English stud, Walter Raleigh,
Was always remarkably jolly,
    Particularly
    When it happened that he
Was in bed with a buxom young dolly.

124. MONOTONOUS

Said a certain delightful old nut,
"I guess I am just in a rut
    Made of breast and of lips
    And vaginas and hips
And sometimes a well-rounded butt."

125. WOMEN'S LIB

A reporter who worked on the journal,
Once said to his girlfriend, "Why, sure, Nell,
    If you don't mind a mess
    Just hike up your dress
And then you can use a man's urinal."

126. COMIC STRIP

A well-known reporter, Clark Kent,
Had a simpering, mild-mannered bent.
    But he grabbed Lois Lane
    And then made it quite plain
What his cognomen, Superman, meant.

1 2 7 . ALL THE WAY

There was a young woman of Brest
Who had a magnificent chest.
    When asked if she posed
    With her nipples disclosed,
She said, "Yes—also all of the rest."

1 2 8 . SEARCH

There was a young woman named Annie
With erogenous zones in each cranny.
    She found this was so
    With the help of her beau,
Who explored her from forehead to fanny.

1 2 9 . TAKE YOUR TURN

There once was a sweet signorina
Who made one quite glad to have seen 'er.
    To get in, however, you
    Had better endeavor to
Wait in line with a legal subpoena.

130. ASTOUNDING

In Venus, where love's an addiction,
An orgasm's brought on by friction
    Of toes against toes,
    Or nose against nose,
And that's what I call science fiction.

131. FIRST TIME

His first night, Adam said to his dear,
"Darling Eve, you had better stand clear.
    Since touched by your hand
    It's begun to expand
And I don't know how far 'twill uprear."

132. COMFORT

Joe was burrowing one day quite nosily
Down the generous cleavage of Rosalie,
    And, what made it more lewd,
    They were both in the nude
So that they could continue more cozily.

1 3 3. TRY IT AGAIN

There was a young fellow of Tulsa,
Who said, "Sex has grown very dull, suh,
    Yet I'm that much a dope,
    If a girl says there's hope
I don't have the heart to repulse 'er."

1 3 4. ANATOMICAL CURIOSITY

A certain young woman named Chris
Said, "How odd that young men stand to piss.
    After all, it's less taxing
    And much more relaxing,
Just to sit down, as I do—like this."

1 3 5. ESSENTIAL POINT

There was a young fellow named Cliff,
Who said with a yawn, "What's the diff?
    I may not be tall
    And my wealth may be small
But a part of me always stays stiff."

136. JAWOHL

A nostalgic stormtrooper named Schmidt
Used a "Nazi sex practices" kit
    Which had boots and a whip
    With a nice metal tip,
And his bride didn't like it a bit.

137. NOW YOU TELL ME

A certain young lass of Algeria
Was reduced to loud wails of hysteria,
    When her escort one night
    Said, "No, miss, honor bright,
My motives are just not ulterior."

138. PERKING UP THE GATHERING

There was a young fellow named Marty
Who at sex was delightfully hearty.
    With a girl, he'd get in her
    On the floor, during dinner,
And it surely enlivened the party.

139. MACHO

Said a certain curmudgeon named Beecham,
"The ladies? Be certain I'll teach 'em
    To do as I please;
    And if too far to seize,
Never fear. I've a part that will reach 'em."

140. OOH, LA, LA

There was a young lady named Mimi
Who said, "Oh, my dear, you should see me
    In bed with two guys.
    Yet that's not the prize,
It's even more pleasant to be me."

141. IT CAN'T HURT

There was a young woman named Frances
Who decided to better her chances
    By cleverly adding
    Appropriate padding
To enlarge all her protuberances.

142. IT'S MORE USEFUL

An intelligent whore from Albania
Read books and grew steadily brainier.
    Yet it wasn't her science
    That brought her male clients
But her quite uncontrolled nymphomania.

143. WATCH OUT!

It was nice, thought a young man named Max,
To find someone's wife, and relax.
    Yet from such situations
    Can arise complications.
Here's her husband! Good heavens, make tracks!

144. JOHN CIARDI AND I

There is something about satyriasis
That arouses psychiatrists' biases,
    But we're both very pleased
    We're in this way diseased
As the damsel who's waiting to try us is.

Limericks: Too Gross

by John Ciardi

* * *

*Dedicated to all the chairmen
(and other drunks) of all the English
Departments I ever roared out a
Saturday night with—and to
all genial lechers, wherever met.*

1 .

There was a young man from Montrose
Who said to a girl, "I propose
    That since time is short
    For affairs of this sort
We begin by removing our clothes."

2 .

There was a young lady who wouldn't.
Her mother had told her she shouldn't.
    When dear mama died
    She felt free. So she tried,
But by then she was so old she couldn't.

3 .

There was a young lady of Mass
Rather lacking, we all thought, in class.
    She would stroll Boston Common
    And whenever she saw men
She'd whimper, "Please, sir, make a pass."

4 ·

There was a young man from Belle Isle
Who said to his girl, "If you'll, I'll."
    "I'm willing," said she,
    "But first I must see
How you look as I walk down the aisle."

5 ·

There once was a smooth-talking Druid
Whose manner of living was luid.
    He'd engage Druid lasses
    In small talk—no passes,
But the first thing they knew they'd been scruid.

6 .

A candidate known for his bulsh
Gave a speech so incredibly fulsh
    That I give you my word
    The like's not been heard
Since Harding, or maybe Cal Culsh.

7 .

There once was a girl from Red Hook
Who said, "Though I could be mistook,
　　One more time ought to do
　　To get me and you
Into Guinness's World Record Book."

8 .

There was a young lady named Wright
Who simply could not sleep at night
　　Because of the ping-
　　Ping-ping of her spring
And the glare of her little red light.

9 .

To his girl said a Cornish marine,
"You've the knobbiest coastline I've seen.
　　'Twould be wonderful sport
　　To put into port
—If the rest of the fleet hadn't been."

1 0 .

There was a young lady named Laura
Whom the mere thought of sex filled with haura.
  You may think that *de trop*,
  But I want you to know
That the pope and his crowd were all faura.

1 1 .

A pious old lady of Brewster
Forgave all who'd ever abewster,
  But flew into a rage
  Time could not assuage
When she thought of one cad who'd refewster.

1 2 .

A horrible brat from Belgravia
Drove his parents to thoughts of Our Savia.
  "By Jesus," they swore,
  "We can't stand much more
Of this son of a bitch's behavia!"

1 3 .

A luscious young R.N. from Florida
Found that doctors just couldn't be horrida.
　　　They pounced on her date
　　　With a young graduate
And stretched her interne in the corrida.

1 4 .

Cleopatra, when sex was still new to her,
Kept buying up young slaves to tutor her.
　　　But the Pharaoh (her dad),
　　　For fear she'd go bad,
Kept rendering them neuterer and neuterer.

1 5 .

There once was a girl from New Haven
Whose pubic hair was not shaven
　　　But missing because
　　　She slept without drawers
Within range of a nest-building raven.

1 6 .

There once was a bra Scottish sentry
Who was standing his post in the entry
    When the queen saw his stature
    And, yielding to nature,
She soon made him one of the gentry.

1 7 .

Said Sophocles, putting his X
To the contract for *Oedipus Rex,*
    "I predict it will run
    Until the Year One,
If the shooting script plays up the sex."

1 8 .

Said a salty old skipper of Wales,
"Number One, it's all right to chew nails.
    It impresses the crew.
    It impresses me too.
But stop spitting holes in the sails."

1 9 .

A fallen young lady of fashion
Gave vents to all sorts of base passion.
Was she scorned? She was not,
For her ways brought a lot
Of highly respectable cash in.

2 0 .

There was a young fellow named Hodge
Who lured girls to his dear-hunting lodge.
Once they were there,
He made them hunt bare.
Serves them right—it's a corny old dodge.

2 1 .

There was a young man from the Nile
Whose amours lacked savoir and style.
He preferred open country
And brazen effrontery
To the wiles of conventional guile.

22.

There was an old lady named Clarke
Who didn't look bad in the dark.
  In the first mists of dawn
  She looked haggard and wan.
In the full light of day she looked—stark!

23.

A young ghost from old Bangladesh
Went out with a girl and got fresh.
  Said she, "I don't mind
  High spirits, you'll find,
But I won't have you come in the flesh."

24.

There was a young lady from Hannibal
Who won local fame as a cannibal
  By eating her mother,
  Her father, her brother,
And her two sisters, Gertrude and Annabel.

2 5 .

There was an old maid from Cape Hatteras
Who found one night pinned to her matteras,
    A short basic list
    Of things she had missed
With a lengthy P.S. of et ceteras.

2 6 .

On her high horse, a lady named Hopper
Declared she would let no man topper.
    Till Freddy the Fink,
    Having plied her with drink,
Slipped her cinch—and did she come a cropper!

2 7 .

There was a young lady named Jo
Who always said, "Thank you, but no,"
    Which is poised and polite
    But never does quite
As well as, "Sure, Buster, let's go."

28.

> There was a young fellow named Phil
> Who was screwing a girl—as boys will.
>   She had a girl's knack
>   For screwing right back.
> The instinct's not easy to kill.

29.

> It took me some time to agree
> To appear in a film about me
>   And my various ex-wives
>   Detailing our sex lives,
> But I did—and they rated it G.

30.

> "My dear unwed mother," said Clancy,
> "Met a bounder who tickled her fancy.
>   Her fancy thus tickled
>   Caused prickles: thus prickled—
> Well, you know the rest. Life is chancy."

31.

There was a young madam, a peach,
Who would lure groups of men from the beach.
    When she got them indoors
    She'd phone various whores
And collect a commission from each.

32.

There was a young fellow named Fred
Who took a young lady to bed,
    Then slept the night through,
    Neglecting to do
What her mother had taught her to dread.

33.

A newly found Latin inscription
Refers to a learned Egyptian
    Who at age CCX
    Still indulged in wild sex
After taking a secret prescription.

34·

Said a learned old man of Brabant,
"The instinct, my dear, is extant:
     The extension's extinct.
     Or to be more succinct:
I would if I could, but I can't."

35·

Said a thrice-tested young man named Landis,
"Don't mourn, dear. You know how a gland is.
     If you'll just use your head,
     You'll find *limp* is not *dead*:
It will still serve *mutatis mutandis*."

36.

An ill-advised salesman named Wade
Made a stop in Kentucky and played
     With a girl in the hay
     Till he heard someone say,
"Step aside, Sis," and "Mistah, yoah daid!"

3 7 .

Our neighborhood whore is no beauty.
But we're not the sort to be snooty.
    We favor a lass
    With a good country ass
And a proper devotion to duty.

3 8 .

There once was a lady named Billie
Who wandered through life willy-nilly
    In aimless affairs
    With chance millionaires
Whose trinkets made marriage look silly.

3 9 .

Said a middle-aged housewife named Pratt,
"Can you damned men think only of *that?*
    Put it back in your pants!"
    "So much for romance,"
Said her husband, "Go shit in your hat!"

4 0.

Slim, the wrangler, went into cahoots
With a girl to indulge in pursuits
    Unchaste and clandestine
    Which began by divestin'
Themselves of their red union suits.

4 1.

Here lies an old stinker from Stoneham.
I can't say I'm glad to have known 'im—
    He was filthy, a cheat,
    A rat-fink, a dead beat—
But *de mortuis nil nisi bonum.*

4 2.

There was an old geezer who tried
All night long, as a matter of pride.
    By dawn's early light
    He whispered, "Goodnight,"
And went into the bathroom and cried.

4 3 ·

A pointless old miser named Quince
Spent a lifetime in skinning his flints.
    When the last flint was skun
    He said, "Well, that's done,"
And dropped dead, which he's been ever since.

4 4 ·

There's a girl there on Marathon Key
Who gave my pal Flip the V.D.
    Evil ways are a curse.
    Still, it might have been worse:
Had it come heads, it would have been me.

4 5 ·

There was a young lady named Meg
Who liked to put boys up a peg.
    Said she, "I don't mind.
    I like to be kind.
And I hate to see young fellows beg."

46.

A clever young fellow named Taft
Caught his death in a Vietnamese draft.
    His last words were, "Shit,
      I've been shot!" Which shows wit.
I wonder why nobody laughed.

47.

There was a young lady so forward,
Especially when she was borward,
    That passing by chance
      I could see at a glance
She was thinking of something untoward.

48.

There's a poor teeny-bopper in Wichita
Whose parents do nothing but bitchita.
    They want her to wait
      For a good proper mate,
But how can she when she's all a-twichita?

49.

An eager young cop from Latrobe
Was assigned by the DA to probe
    Into organized vice.
    Which he did. But the price
Was the worst case of pustules since Job.

50.

There was a young man with a rod
Who thought he'd been chosen by God
    To exercise Hell
    From the girls. He meant well,
But the Thunder said: "*Exorcise*—clod!"

51.

There once was a girl from Haw Creek
Whose virtue left something to seek.
    Our young men all sought it
    And most of them bought it,
Though some only came by to peek.

52.

> There was a young fellow named Spiegel
> Who had an affair with a seagull
> What's worse—do you see?—
> It wasn't a she
> But a he-gull—and *that* is illegal.

53.

> There once was a startled young Syrian
> Who coming home late, and who peering in
> The window to coo
> To his wife, beheld two
> Rather lithe Lebanese disappearyin'.

54.

> There was a young lady who knew
> She had chosen the wrong thing to do.
> But she did it so well
> She owned a hotel
> In Miami before she was through.

55.

A spritely young lady named Wise
One midsummer evening gave rise
    To a chain of events
    Involving six gents
In a general unzipping of flies.

56.

There once was a girl—a humdinger—
Around whom the boys liked to linger
    While babbling of love,
    But got nowhere. "Go shove!"
She would say as she gave them the finger.

57.

At Fred's flat a bouncy young whore
Started bouncing about on the floor.
    "That does it!" said Fred.
    "Now you've busted the bed!"
And dismounted. And showed her the door.

58.

There was an old fellow from Keene
Who dropped dead betwixt and between
    Two bundles of hay
    On each of which lay
What New Hampshiremen call a "sireen."

59.

That efficient young harlot at Gorms
Made us fill out "New Customer Forms"
    On "Position desired . . . . .
    Equipment required . . . ."
And "Other (State Norms and Ab-
    norms . . . .)."

60.

There was a young lady from Putney
Who was given to sexual gluttony.
    Warned a pious old duffer,
    "Your morals will suffer."
"That's what you think," she said. "I ain't gutney."

6 1.

An antichurch harlot named Rhonda
Keeps tempting our young monks to wander
From true rectitude
By walking in nude
And saying, "Behold thy Golconda!"

6 2.

A dashing young fellow from Alder
Used to spiel such a pure line of folder-
O-leary-o-lie,
Our maids would near die.
But time passed and his dash became balder.

6 3.

Remember the night in Shanghai
When we put down two gallons of rye
And all eight of the ladies
At Singapore Sadie's?
—How the days of our youth hurry by!

64.

There was a young lady of parts.
Not one of your lower-class tarts—
    She had worked at St. Johns
    Under ten learned dons
And been certified Mistress of Arts.

65.

A bellhop I met in D.C.
Got all his sex services free.
    He patrolled corridors
    Simply tapping on doors
And replying, "Hell, honey, it's me!"

66.

Said the dean, "I don't care what you think
Of the depths to which others may sink,
    But when I go down
    And you tell the whole town
That I did, then, young man—you're a fink!"

67.

Sir, the chef's in a bit of a stew.
When that waitress at post number 2
    Comes into the kitchen
    He's so busy hitchin'
His pants, that he burns the ragout.

68.

A middle-aged lady named Brewer
Used to ask all the fellows to do her
    A favor of sorts,
    But the number of sports
Who were willing grew fewer and fewer.

69.

There was a masseuse at the club
Who was giving a member a rub.
    Said the member, rubbed red,
    "Please, miss, use your head—
You're rubbing me down to a nub!"

70.

There once was a learned guru
Who found he had nothing to do,
    So he sat on a tack
    And thought into and back
And out and beyond—and clear through.

71.

There once was a stripper who stripped
Until she was barely equipped.
    Said she in chagrin
    As she fingered her skin,
"Good heaven's—this part of it's ripped!"

72.

There was an ex-Wave with a suite
Overlooking the Bay. When the fleet
    Steamed in from maneuvers
    She blinked with her louvers,
"Standing by to be boarded. Repeat:
Standing by to be boarded. Repeat:
Standing by to be boarded. Repeat . . ."

7 3 ·

Said her grace, "I impose one condition
Before I assume the position.
　　It's my view that nudity
　　Cannot excuse crudity.
No fucking. Just tasteful coition."

7 4 ·

There was a young lady named Stein
With rondures so nearly divine
　　And so few inhibitions
　　To set harsh conditions,
That she spent half her life on her spine.

7 5 ·

P.S.　The rest of her time, let me add,
　　Was not spent in cleaning her pad,
　　　　But prone, or asprawl,
　　　　Or astraddle, but all—
　　Nearly all of it—scantily clad.

76.

Which saved her a deal of expense.
Thus, by practicing good common sense,
    She made both ends meet
    Though the rent of her suite,
And her lingerie bills, were immense.

77.

There was an old lecherous earl
Who took in a poor homeless girl
    And induced her to sin
    With promises, gin,
And such cant as "Let's give it a whirl!"

78.

There was a young lady named Rose
Who liked to slip out of her clothes
    When receiving a gent,
    Which helped pay the rent
And kept her amused, I suppose.

79.

There was a young lady named Rose
Who liked to slip out of her clothes
    When men came to call.
    "You are welcome to all,"
She would say, striking pose after pose.

80.

Vicar Smedley, our pie-in-the-sky man
Called on Clara and ruptured her hymen
    On the eve of her marriage
    To Tredlowe T. Claridge—
Which I'd say is rather shrewd timin'.

81.

A drunken old tar from Saint Clements,
To ward off the scurvy, sucked lemons.
    "With my health unimpaired,
    I have time," he declared,
"To die of delirium tremens."

82.

A personnel person from Cobb
Was giving a young man the job.
    Said she, "I can tell
    You will do very well.
You're a young man who uses his knob."

83.

There was a young lady from Lester
Who allowed all the boys to molest her.
    She was gentle and kind,
    But those traits, you may find,
Spread diseases that burn, itch, and fester.

84.

As Dame Eleanor came through the door,
Her chambermaid leaped from the floor,
    Interrupting coition.
    "What a curious position!"
Said the dame, "May I see it once more?"

8 5 .

A young mountain climber named Frazier
Fell into a crack in a glacier.
    "This is really appalling!"
    He shouted while falling,
Then lapsed into total aphasia.

8 6 .

There was a young lady from Brest
Whom the curé once put to the test
    By letting her see
    How bleak sin could be,
But she wasn't the least bit impressed.

8 7 .

"Yes, of course," said a girl from Latrop,
"But it's hard to know quite where to stop.
    A boy lifts your slip.
    Then you hear him unzip.
Then what do you do?—call a cop?"

8 8 .

> There was a young fellow so poor
> He lived in a half-furnished sewer.
>> He never complained
>> Though at times—when it rained—
> He did find life hard to endure.

8 9 .

> At the Pan-Hell Olympics last week
> The second prize went to a Deke.
>> Amid mounting applause
>> From the third-place Psi Taus
> He laid eighteen girls cheek to cheek.

9 0 .

> There's a lady in suite 7-C
> Who allowed two young men to make free
>> Till she heard someone say,
>> "That's all for today."
> And discovered she'd been on TV.

9 1.

There was a young lady whose taste
Ran to chain mail and locks 'round the waist.
    She was charming, I'd say,
    In a general way,
But rather obsessively chaste.

9 2.

An insomniac young fellow named Hatches
Took a room in a whorehouse in Natchez.
    He still tossed and turned
    Half the night, but he learned
How to manage by sleeping in snatches.

9 3.

A widow of some fashion kept
A young lout in her bed while she slept.
    She would smile when she woke
    To finger his spoke,
And think, "This lacks couth, but it's ept."

94·

Said Socrates, keeping his poise,
"Tell Xanthippe I've done with her noise.
      If she asks what you mean,
      Just say, when last seen
I was drinking with some of the boys."

95·

On the talk show last night, Dr. Ellis,
The sex shrink, took two hours to tell us
      It's all right to enjoy
      A rosy-cheeked boy
So long as your sheep don't get jealous.

96.

There was a stout lad of the fleet
In Cherbourg, in the chips, and in heat.
      He bought out La Maison
      De Madame de Bonbon,
And kept calling for girls toot-de-sweet.

9 7 ·

There was a male chauvinist pig
Who bought a stuffed bra and a wig
    And started rehearsin'
    To be a chairperson
In case Bella Abzug won big.

9 8 .

One dark night a lady from Snelling
Awoke with a curious swelling
    In the palm of her hand.
    It was—yes—a male gland.
But whose, she had no way of telling.

9 9 ·

There once was a diddlesome lass
Whose dandles drew young men *en masse*.
    What with diddling and dandling
    She endured much manhandling—
Rather more than most girls of her class.

1 0 0 .

There once was a girl who used paint
On her navel. Her boyfriend said, "Ain't
      That going too far?"
      "No more than you are,"
She said. "Do I hear a complaint?"

1 0 1 .

There was a young man at Twin Lakes
With a terrible case of the shakes.
      He writhed on the lawn
      From midnight to dawn
Like Laocoön, but with more snakes.

1 0 2 .

A young baseball groupie named Ritter
Will soon need a good babysitter.
      She couldn't say no
      To the sluggers, and so
She got hit, but she can't say what hitter.

103.

Said an airy young lady from Metz
Who kept ordering more crêpes suzettes,
   "Of course I don't eat them
   But nothing can beat them
For a posh way to light cigarettes."

104.

Have you heard about Mrs. Cotell?
She checked into the Eden Motel
   For a blissful weekend
   With the friend of a friend,
But when she got home she caught Hell.

105.

There was a young wife from Peoria
Who checked into the Waldorf-Astoria
   Where she stayed for a week
   With two Swedes and a Greek
In a state of near-total euphoria.

106.

Said Miguel to the gringo, "Señor,
Eef I open these here closet door,
    An' dee lady eenside
    Ees my leetle lost bride,
Than I theenk I mus' shoot you some more."

107.

Said a girl who was forced to go dutch
On a love nest, "I don't mind too much.
    Though I pay half the lease,
    I collect half—apiece—
From Smitty, Gil, Stu, Tim, and Hutch."

108.

Said Calpurnia, "Though I must render
Unto Caesar the brunt of my gender,
    A few side effects
    Are permitted my sex
When we're feeling illegally tender."

109.

There was a young fellow from Bingham
Whose girl had to run off and bring 'im
    A new set of tweeds
    While he hid in the weeds
Where he'd lost his while jigging her thingum.

110.

A toast to the lady vice cop
With the most busts for trying to stop
    The tide of ill-doing
    In pay-for-play screwing—
Undercover, she came out on top!

111.

"Yes, mother, it's starting to show,"
Said Nell, "But no use blaming Joe.
    And I doubt it was Fred,
    Or the vicar, or Ned.
The fact is, I simply don't know."

1 1 2 .

"Is it too much to ask," said Lord Rayne
To a baggage with whom he had lain,
    "That you wait below stairs
    And tend your affairs,
In case I require you again?"

1 1 3 .

What a temperate man Dr. Wise is.
When three coeds in silly disguises
    Leaped on him in bed,
    He did not scold. He said,
"Very well, then. But no more surprises!"

1 1 4 .

There was a young fellow named Shear
Who stuck a ballpoint in his ear.
    When he punctured the drum
    He said, "That hurts some,
But the rest of the way through is clear."

1 1 5 .

Said a wicked old madam named Belle
Whom the preacher was threatening with Hell,
    "I have no regrets,
     No doubts—and no debts.
If I haven't done good, I've done well."

1 1 6 .

There once was an Arab so poor
He was forced by the neighborhood whore
    To trade his left nut
     For a night with the slut,
Who dried it to hang on her door.

1 1 7 .

The Tri-Delts are under a cloud.
When their housemother, Mrs. Van Dowd,
    Either quit or retired,
     They seem to have hired
A stripteaser—which isn't allowed.

1 1 8 .

> There was a young pilot from Bangor
> Who locked eighteen girls in his hangar
> > Where he treated them wrong
> > And kept them so long
> The countryside rose up in anger.

1 1 9 .

> A conservative lady named Tabor
> Had a date with her radical neighbor.
> > They argued all night
> > On the left and the right.
> In the end, though, he brought her to labor.

1 2 0 .

> There once was a girl from Bermuda
> Who undressed till she couldn't be nuda.
> > When one young man inquired
> > Why she wasn't attired,
> She said, "Can't you be a bit cruda?"

1 2 1 .

A young public steno from Surrey
Did her work well with never a worry.
    Though her clients were myriad
    She did not miss a period,
For she never did things in a hurry.

1 2 2 .

A shepherd who came from Bangkok
Used to dabble in watered-down stock.
    His peculiar perversion
    Was total immersion
Till he drowned all the sheep in his flock.

1 2 3 .

There was a young lady named Candy
Who made do, when no boys were handy,
    With a girlfriend or two—
    Sometimes Betty Lou,
But more often Belinda and Mandy.

1 2 4 .

> Said a hesitant youth from Siberia,
> "If it please you to, uh, try, my dearie, uh,
>   This, uh, thingumbob
>   Is what, uh, does the job
> When it's thrust into, uh, your interia."

1 2 5 .

> An efficient young lady of Rome
> Began to do piecework at home.
>   Eight hours a day,
>   Fifteen minutes a lay,
> Neatly timed by the chimes from the Dome.

1 2 6 .

> A young handyman from Biloxi
> Tried coating his tool with epoxy.
>   In practice he found—
>   Though his theory was sound—
> It was rather like screwing by proxy.

1 2 7 .

"No! No!" said a man so penurious
He'd convinced himself sex was injurious,
    "At a pretty a penny
    I wouldn't have any.
At tuppence, I'm not even curious."

1 2 8 .

There was a magician named Carr
Who used to be billed as a star.
    His future looked sweet
    Till he walked down the street
And—*presto!*—turned into a bar.

1 2 9 .

A wandering minstrel named Gay
Got a girl in the family way.
    Her brother and dad
    Rode after the cad.
And that was the minstrel's last lay.

130.

There was a young devil named Stu
Who ruined a maiden or two.
    That is, if good screwin'
    Can cause a girl's ruin.
Even so—give the devil his due.

131.

The late poet Wystan Hugh Aud'n
Left us poems never maudl'n but mod'n.
    The first things he wrote
    Struck a socialist note,
But increasingly then he let God'n.

132.

I know an old harlot named Triskett
So broad in the rump and the brisket
    That since she began
    To solicit, no man
Has said "Let's go!" but only "I'll risk it!"

133.

There was a young fellow from Kent
Who drank till he grew redolent.
    He wasn't so rank
    You could quite say he stank,
But downwind he gave off quite a scent.

134.

I don't give a damn, by and large,
About sex. There's too much persiflage
    In dating and bedding
    And, worst of all, wedding.
It just doesn't give me a charge.

135.

There was a young man of Des Moines
Who made rather too much of his groin.
    "Make a bid," he would shout
    As he flashed it about.
"OK, Ladies—Going . . . going . . . goin'!"

136.

> I doubt that much more will be heard
> Of Agatha Margaret MacBird.
> > She was last seen in Berks
> > With two businesslike Turks
> Who were peddling her off to a third.

137.

> There was a young fellow named Pfister
> Who noticed an odd sort of blister
> > Where no blister should be.
> > What was worse—do you see?—
> He had got it at home from his sister.

138.

> I was told by a mathematician
> That the odds against having coition
> > With Betty Jo Donne
> > Are a hundred to one.
> So they are—till you ask her permission.

1 3 9.

A pious young maiden named Dexter
Prayed so long that it damn near desexed 'er.
    Yet, though she prayed hard,
    Her mind, when off guard,
Churned up visions that vexed and perplexed 'er.

1 4 0.

There once was an upcoming lad.
Full of juice, but a bit of a cad.
    Once he got off his rocks
    He would put on his socks
And sneer, "Well, I guess you've been had!"

1 4 1.

A devout but ambiguous maid
Liked to play with the boys. Having played
    She feared (some) for her soul
    But believed on the whole
She was not lost but only mislaid.

1 4 2 .

> I feel sorry for young Dr. Dow.
> Our ladies won't go to him now.
>> When examining the parts
>> Of Mrs. Ray Hartz
> He should have said "Hmmm" and not "Wow!"

1 4 3 .

> I said to the neighborhood whore,
> "How's my credit?" She showed me the door.
>> It gets hard for a bloke
>> When he's friendless and broke,
> But I guess that's the fate of the poor.

1 4 4 .

> At a serious bar in Bel Air
> A lady walked in and stood bare.
>> She kept leering and winking.
>> But drinking is drinking,
> And not one man noticed her there.

1 4 5 ·

There was a young lady from Rye
Who was roundly misused by a guy.
    She did not feel abused
    At being so used.
She was happy to give it a try.

1 4 6 ·

There was a young lady named Burr
Who, when dating, wore nothing but fur.
    When she slipped off her coat
    She would say—and I quote—
"I hope I am causing a stir."

1 4 7 · *

Said a voice from the back of the car,
"Young man, I don't know who you are.
    But allow me to state,
    Though it may come too late,
I had not meant to go quite this far."

---

* PUBLISHER'S NOTE:
Mr. Ciardi appears to have cheated and gone over his gross limit.
In his defense let it be noted that the three extras are little more
than addenda, or explanations, or variations, or warts on three
others of his collection.